THE CREATIVE PRAYER JOURNAL

A 21-Day Prayer Challenge to Experiencing
Meaningful Conversations With God

Kim C. Steadman

Lifter Upper

Grand Prairie, TX

Kim Steadman
P.O. Box 543211
Grand Prairie, TX 75054

To learn more about the author, visit www.KimSteadman.com

ISBN-10: 0-9983419-1-6

ISBN-13: 978-0-9983419-1-0

Printed in the United States of America

Scripture quotations marked (WEB) are taken from the World English Bible, public domain.

Scripture quotations marked (KJV) are taken from the King James Version, public domain.

Scripture quotations marked (ASV) are taken from the American Standard Version, public domain.

www.TheCreativePrayerJournal.com

Acknowledgments

Does every little girl dream about writing a book? I did. I thought about it as I curled up on my canopy bed reading stories or playing "library" with my dolls. I have to thank my parents, Sue and Steve for instilling in me the love of books and learning. I'll never take for granted their faith in me and my abilities.

I want to also thank my husband, Stan, for your support, believing in me, and your encouragement. Thank you for loving me first. I love you a ba-ga-zillion+1.

To my son, Matthew, I thank you for your love. No matter your age, you'll always be my baby and I'll always love you.

To my grandson, Rusty, you are the reason why I write. Meme loves you bunches and bunches.

I dedicate this book to my great-grandmother, Eppie Vaughn. She gave to her heirs the most valuable legacy anyone could bestow:

The example of her unwavering faithfulness to her Lord and Savior, Jesus Christ.

The wealth of an overflowing heart full of an unconditional love.

The treasure of prayers for all her family and friends. She was the epitome of being a prayer warrior.

Shout and Shine, Granny! Shout and Shine!

Table of Contents

Introduction

Welcome to this 21-day journey towards meaningful, effective and creative personal prayer time. I am so excited that you have decided to join us in this challenge. Creative prayer ideas are methods and prompts used as interesting approaches to daily personal prayer.

Prayer is vital to knowing God and our spiritual growth just as eating and breathing is to staying alive. As you go through this challenge you will be keeping a prayer journal. You can keep your journal in this book or a spiral notebook, composition book, or online.

I encourage you to commit your heart to the next 21 days of this creative prayer journal challenge. Each day you will read an entry in the book and follow that day's idea for writing in your prayer journal. If you miss a day, don't give up. Start where you left off and continue.

You can visit www.KimSteadman.com/study to find some bonus goodies such as an accountability checklist, coloring pages, and a prayer study guide suitable for a three week personal or group Bible study.

Thank you for joining me on this prayer journey. God bless you!

Kim

Chapter One:
Why Pray?

Prayer isn't magic fairy dust we sprinkle around to entice God or order Him to do something. It's much deeper because prayer is communicating with and hearing from God. Therefore, when our will is in line with God's will, then we enter a time of sincere prayer. It's our connection to heaven–and the communication line is a two-way street! Recent statistics at www.Pewforum.com say 55% of Americans continue to say they pray at least once a day. But, the share of U.S. adults who seldom or never pray has increased from 18% to 23% since 2007. The increase in the statistic saddens me because so many are missing out open communication with God.

But, I'll be the first to admit I'm not the perfect prayer warrior. I've faltered and stumbled in my faith and my prayer walk. So, you can trust me when I say I don't feel worthy to write any book teaching others to pray.

Then, what brought me to this place of writing a book to teach others creative prayer ideas? In fact, what are creative prayer ideas? My definition is "creative prayer ideas are methods, ideas, and prompts used as interesting approaches to daily personal prayer."

I wrote this book after personal reflection of the last two years. Through a series of certain events, I found myself retired in early 2015. That was the kind way of putting I ditched my 9 to 5 job with a **1-month resignation letter**. Once vibrant, happy and full of life, I had now become a worn out shell. Physical, mental and spiritual burnout was sickening my body.

Several stresses for the past four years had accumulated and included:

- I launched a new career within the company I had worked at for 16 years.
- I entered peri-menopause. I didn't know it could start in my 40's!
- Mother had two strokes in December 2012.
- Along with my husband, I continued a more active role in taking care of the family property.
- We continued ministering at our church and working full-time jobs.
- The most heart wrenching was that in late 2014 our adult son attempted suicide.

By January of 2015, I was putting one foot in front of the other and living a self-absorbed life. By pushing people away, except for my closest family, I cocooned myself. Along with that protective cocoon to keep others out, I had a tendency to have an over-active stress response to events both personal and work related.

Just as physical burnout always has a cause, so does a spiritual exhaustion. I knew the answer to my physical exhaustion. Long days, lack of rest, overwhelming stress, an overweight body, an under-active lifestyle and poor eating habits hurt my body. But, can any other woman relate? After all, it's hard maintaining the role of a superwoman!

Additionally, my spiritual burnout list was long. But I could trace to the taproot on this one. Have you heard of a taproot? A carrot is a taproot. When you eat a crunchy, orange carrot, you are eating the root. If you've ever grown them or bought a bunch at the organic market, you will notice little, hairy fiber roots on the sides. The hairy roots are important, but the taproot is the central, life-giving part of the plant which happens to be edible. The taproot to my spiritual burnout was that I had been guilty of letting my prayer life grow stale.

4

After all, I prayed every day. But, my prayers were a list of my needs and wants and repeats of yesterday's prayers. I hate to admit it, but a personal prayer time wasn't even on my daily schedule. I'm sure my daily prayers asking God part the cars so we could get home faster didn't count as a meaningful prayer. My spirit was dry and cracked, but God's grace surrounded me during my time of prayer drought.

When I quit, I explained to people I was going home to restore and heal my body, heart, mind and soul. I came back to my peaceful sanctuary and took the first year to concentrate on restoring the four, life-giving elements of mind, body, heart and soul. Yes, my heart and soul needed restoration, and I used prayer. What did I mean by restoring? Did I have a plan? I didn't have an answer. But I traveled down a road to discovery. My personal prayer time became one of the paths in the journey.

This book isn't defending prayer. I will assume you believe in prayer. This book isn't meant to convince you that prayer works. I will make another assumption you think prayer works. I feel that you crave a more meaningful personal prayer time. You are looking for ways, ideas, and prompts to get you there. That's what I've written for you. The thoughts, journey, methods and modes I used to restore meaningful conversations to God into my life.

So, I ask you:

- Are you looking for personal prayer time rejuvenation?
- Are you a busy woman who can't cram even the important things into her daily schedule including daily prayer time?
- Do you disengage from praying by becoming bored or your mind wanders with a list you need to do?
- Is your life stressed by taking care of career needs and family needs?
- Do you find you pray more for yourself than for others?
- Are you living a stressed life that leaves you tired, even too tired to pray?
- Is your spirit burdened with your needs, you find it hard to pray for others when you pray?
- Do you have your prayer list, but you still flounder with what to pray?

- Are you confused with your current life events and want guidance?
- Do you pray lots of prayers that start or end with the words 'why God?'
- Is your faith weak and you are looking to prayer to strengthen it?
- Is your faith strong and you want meaningful prayer to increase it?
- Do you sometimes struggle with the right words to say when you pray?
- Does your mind wander when you pray?

If you answered yes to any of these questions, then know you aren't alone. I've been where you are. Using the prayer ideas in this book, I restored joy, fervency, and meaning to my prayer life. Now it's time for you to redefine your prayer life and lose the baggage of prayer problems.

Chapter Two:
Creative and Fun Prayers

As a child, you learned different ways to pray. For example, simple childhood prayers used for mealtime or bedtime may have been a daily routine. But somewhere along the line, adults get a crazy notion that prayers should be formal with flowery words; some even want to sound poetic in their flow of words like the Psalmist or the writer of Songs of Solomon. The perception is they should be speech worthy. Such a mindset hinders your prayers. You may be thinking about the right posture to adopt in prayer. Should you hang up on your body's position? Should you sit, be on your knees, or stand? What's right, and is one wrong? Questions keep you stuck in the legalities. Rituals get in the way. Prayer meant to be straightforward and pure becomes legalistic.

While many women enjoy sufficient prayer using lists, I find them annoying. Are Christians **allowed to say the words annoyed and prayer** in the **same** sentence? Well, I did, and God didn't strike me with a bolt of lightning! Another example of a prayer formats is the intricate and organized prayer binders with dividers, but those were overwhelming to me. As a result, my prayers had become a litany of names and needs. But, I wanted a deeper, more meaningful daily prayer time with the lover of my soul. I literally desired romance (if you don't mind that word) with God in my heart of heart—something that takes me *into* Him.

I was in the middle of a project for my mom. I had collected and recollected prayer ideas when I was looking into creating a prayer format for her. Mom is a four-year stroke survivor. While the stroke didn't take her life, she became another stroke statistic with short-term memory problems. Unfortunately, she had a hard time concentrating during prayer. Remembering people's names and needs had become difficult along with staying focused during prayer time.
I developed a fill-in-the-blank format (included in this book) to help her prayer journey. In the course of this, my personal prayer journey started too. It started because of the simple word that stuck with me-*fun*. I had fun. As a result, I prayed more and longed for the personal time with God using the format I developed for her. I realized my prayers didn't need to be deeper. What I needed was a personal prayer time with fewer lists and more writing of God-inspired thoughts, along with variety such as worship, quietness, and meditation.

What I discovered was that several of those "children's" prayer ideas changed me. Even though years ago, I taught little ones in Sunday School all these things, I began to use them more in my personal prayer life. As a result, I rediscovered power, joy, and commitment to prayer. I decided prayer could be fun and exciting! In essence, I realized that personal prayer time isn't one of **those one sizes fits everyone** shawls. You may need variety and an original format to call your own. It could be these fun prayer journal ideas!

Sometimes you'll need formal prayers, but your everyday prayer life doesn't have to be a regimented list. If predictability and cookie-cutter prayer formats are leaving you dry, thirsty, and skipping daily conversation with your Heavenly Father, then it's time for a change. You see, God doesn't want to be unfamiliar to you. He longs to hear your voice. He intends to be as real to you as a loved one sitting across the room from you, and He wants your prayers like a heart-to-heart conversation between friends.

Nevertheless, sometimes a conversation is difficult. Memory loss (such as my mom's struggle) or stressed, busy minds can cause the heart and mind to become disconnected. I've been in seasons of time where stress made praying hard. Please know that if you've had those severe moments or years of stress, then I know your struggles-I've gone through the cycle, too. That's why these simple, prayer journal ideas are the best thing I've added to my prayer life.

These 21 ideas are the tip of the iceberg. It's a simple start when it comes to the first step in restoring and developing an original and meaningful prayer time in your life.

I invite you to join me on a 21-day prayer journey. You'll be writing, gluing, and walking through a Word-full and prayerful journey! Grab a hot cup of hot tea, your prayer journal in hand, and your Bible. Let your prayers be fun as you create meaningful conversations with God.

Gather Your Supplies

There are so many types of prayer journals that you can create and make to suit your personal taste. I can get lost for hours looking at places like Google and Pinterest for ideas. For this book and its ideas, I wanted to get back to the basics—the easy, the simple. When life is at its most stressful state for me (and my mom), simplicity has been our friend. So, your supply list is short and sweet.

Supply List

Journal: Any journal will do. You may already have a special journal you want to use. It may be hard cover or softcover, pretty or plain, bound or spiral. The most important thing is to buy a journal that you will write in. I'm always amazed when I look at my shelf of unused journals because I'm ever waiting for that special time to write in them. That's why nowadays my favorite journal is a simple composition book or spiral notebook. If you don't like the cover, you can cut out some pretty pictures and use some Modgepodge glue to cover it.

Pen or Pencil: If you want to write permanently and are confident about what you write, then you'll need a pen—maybe in a fun color too. If you think you'll want to be able to erase unwanted or excess content along the way, then you'll need a pencil or an erasable pen.

9

Now, before we go into the prayer ideas, take in the following hints, which have helped me to have a meaningful prayer time. They will help you get the best out of what you're about to learn.

Do one thing at a time: Your brain has to choose what to remember. Having a designated 'prayer time' will help to filter out what you want to think about and remember. Find your quiet place—away from distractions—in any part of your home. It doesn't have to be your room. You may want to have it in your garden while the kids are at home because you can't be praying and be talking to the little ones at the same time. Give God His time and give your family their time.

Fully concentrate: Don't think about what you are going to have for the next meal. Don't have a lot of background noise like the television or radio. Fully concentrate on your prayer time. It will help you to have a more meaningful prayer time.

Say it out loud: Science has proven that when you repeat things out loud, you will be able to remember them. Hearing your own voice helps you to remember such things. Applying that same principle to your prayer life helps too. You'll find that names and needs come to your mind easily, thus you won't feel so 'empty' when you want to pray. After you've written in your prayer journal, it helps to read it out loud too.

Write it down: The act of writing something requires concentration. There was a study called "The Pen is Mightier Than the Keyboard." It showed that writing things down are still the best way to not only learn something new but also remember it later. That's one of the reasons I created a prayer journal idea for my mom, which was called the "PrayerFULL prayer template." By writing down names and needs in a creative format, you are connecting your mind and your heart through the process of prayer.

Chapter Three:
The Creative Prayer Journal

The following 21 days are designed to take you on a multi-sensory prayer experience. You pray in a different format on each day. The day may be composed of writing, drawing, walking, thanking, praising and meditating or a combination.

I've provided you with a theme scripture to start your day followed by prompts and instructions. There is space in the journal for you to write, or you may choose to write in a separate journal of your own.

My hope is you find yourself renewed with these creative prayer ideas. My prayer is for you and yours to be blessed.

Day 1...
Be PrayerFULL

"This is the boldness which we have toward him, that, if we ask anything according to his will, he listens to us." (1 John 5:14, WEB)

I've taught this format under a different acronym. I renamed some of the elements to keep aligned with my mission of helping my mom to have a more prayerFULL life. Here is the format I used when I created prayer journal pages for her:

F - Focus on God

U - Utterly rely on God's forgiveness

L - Let your requests be known

L - Let's give thanks

Focus On God:

First, you will have to "Focus on God." The Lord's Prayer starts with the words *Our Father*. Christ has shown us that we should begin our prayers with a focus on God, our Heavenly Father.

Most of us know what a father is. At the most basic, a father is the person that is 50% responsible for your life. Then there is the emotional level. Some of us had a wonderful, loving, caring father here on earth. Others may not have beautiful memories of what a father is. We'll go to the scriptures and Greek to help us understand what Christ meant when He said "Our Father."

The Greek word for Father is 'Pater, ' and it means 'one who imparts life and commits to it.' Our Heavenly Father is not only our Creator but commits to active participation in our life (if we allow Him.) He's the giver of both of our lives-our physical and our spiritual birth into eternal life.

We inherit certain aspects of our physical (biological) father at the microscopic level of our DNA. We also inherit physical aspects such as the color of eyes or the shapes of our nose. Later as we grow someone may say to us "You're acting just like your father." As we grow in our knowledge of God, our actions should also resemble our Heavenly Father.

Start your prayer time by writing down one word or small phrase that describes God. Pray, "God, you are _____."

Utterly Rely On God's Forgiveness:

But if you stop and let the air out, you can then refill it again and again. Asking God's forgiveness is like letting the air out so that you can refill with good air!

Say, "God, forgive me of_____. And I forgive _____ (mention names) of _____ (mention the offenses) and I release, send away and omit them."

Let Your Requests Be Known:

The Lord's Prayer has six petitions. The first three relate to God. The last three relate to us as to our daily needs, the forgiveness of our sins, and our deliverance from evil. He does want us to think about our prayers and our needs. I remember when I was young and the Sears Christmas Catalog would arrive our home. I would carefully go through the big book and eventually mark things that I would like for Christmas, even though there was no guarantee that I would get them. But, I carefully thought about my requests. Christ patterned for us the care and thought we should put into our prayers.
Say, "God, I need _____."

Let's Give Thanks:

The Lord's Prayer doesn't include specific instructions about thankfulness. But we do find other places in the Scriptures where we are to be thankful. They center on your response to what is in your life, that is–the prayers already answered, those that are unanswered, and the daily blessings that you might have taken for granted. While there is a difference between prayer and thanksgiving the two are also related. Your Christian walk will deepen as you learn to give thanks, even while you have unanswered prayers. "In everything give thanks...." (1 Thessalonians 5:18).

Reflections

Day 2...
Pray The News

"In nothing be anxious, but in everything, by prayer and petition with thanksgiving, let your requests be made known to God. And the peace of God, which surpasses all understanding, will guard your hearts and your thoughts in Christ Jesus." (Philippians 4:6-7, WEB)

There are many ways to hear the daily news in these modern days. You may get your news topics on a social media site, a major news site, independent news media, a magazine or in the old fashioned newspaper. Whatever your source may be, I'm sure there are days that you feel like there's a lot to pray about. There is.

For the news you watch or read from any given sources, write a corresponding point of prayer according to each of the news items. You can take five minutes to pray the news or you could easily pray all day (let your heart guide you).

I would make a note in this one about those people that have an empathetic nature. If you are anything like me, this prayer will fill you with a deep burden, and tire you. I can only pray this type of prayer about one day a week. Unfortunately we live in a time of turmoil right now and there is no lack of bad news out there. I live in a large city between two major cities characterized with high crime rates and horrific things in the news. Therefore, let the Lord guide you. After the 21-day challenge, if you find you can't pray this type of prayer multiple days in a row don't be discouraged. There are many other ways to pray.

Reflections

Day 3...
Copy a Prayer

Copy a prayer that someone else prayed. Writing the prayer in your handwriting can help you connect your heart with your mind for internal oneness and concentration. To get yourself started here is a suggested list of effective prayers that have had an impact on the world:

The Lord's Prayer (Matthew 6:9-13)
The disciples asked Jesus to teach them to pray. In response, Jesus gave them the most fundamental of all prayers-the prayer of hope for the soul that is tied to our Heavenly Father. In the request "Lord, teach us to pray," Jesus gives them the fundamental Christian prayer-the prayer of hope.

"Our Father, which art in heaven,

Hallowed be thy Name.

Thy Kingdom come.

Thy will be done in earth,

As it is in heaven.

Give us this day our daily bread.

And forgive us our trespasses,

As we forgive them that trespass against us.

And lead us not into temptation,

But deliver us from evil.

For thine is the kingdom,

The power, and the glory,

For ever and ever.

Amen."

(From the Anglican Book of Common Prayer, 1662).

St. Patrick's Prayer

"Christ with me,

Christ before me,

Christ behind me,

Christ in me,

Christ beneath me,

Christ above me,

Christ on my right,

Christ on my left,

Christ when I lie down,

Christ when I sit down,

Christ when I arise,

Christ in the heart of every man who thinks of me,

Christ in the mouth of everyone who speaks of me,

Christ in every eye that sees me,

Christ in every ear that hears me."

William Tyndall and His Prayer for the King of England

William Tyndall's passionate mission was that everyone should have access to the Bible. He lived during a time when only the priests of the church had a Latin copy. Servants and regular folks didn't have a copy of their own. He was a scholar who could speak both Hebrew and Greek, and he gave his life fighting for the right that all souls should have a copy of the Bible in the English language. Just before he was put to death, he exclaimed to the crowd,

"Lord, open the King of England's eyes!"

It's a beautiful prayer to write when you have a burdened heart for those whose eyes need to open. You can insert their name(s) in the place of the words "the King of England's."

Say, "Lord, open _____'s eyes."

Dr. Kent M. Keith's - The Paradoxical Commandments

While this isn't a prayer, it's thoughts we have all had. Dr. Keith wrote these commandments as part of the second chapter of his booklet, "The Silent Revolution: Dynamic Leadership in the Student Council" which he wrote for high school student leaders.

> *1. People are illogical, unreasonable, and self-centered. Love them anyway.*

> *2. If you do good, people will accuse you of selfish ulterior motives. Do good anyway.*

> *3. If you are successful, you win false friends and true enemies. Succeed anyway.*

4. The good you do today will be forgotten tomorrow. Do good anyway.

5. Honesty and frankness make you vulnerable. Be honest and frank anyway.

6. The biggest men and women with the biggest ideas can be shot down by the smallest men and women with the smallest minds. Think big anyway.

7. People favor underdogs but follow only top dogs. Fight for a few underdogs anyway.

8. What you spend years building may be destroyed overnight. Build anyway.

9. People really need help but may attack you if you do help them. Help people anyway.

10. Give the world the best you have and you'll get kicked in the teeth. Give the world the best you have anyway.

Mother Teresa adopted his commandments into her "Do It Anyway Prayer" which were found written on the wall in her home for children in Calcutta, India.

1. People are often unreasonable, irrational, and self-centered. Forgive them anyway.

2. If you are kind, people may accuse you of selfish, ulterior motives. Be kind anyway.

3. If you are successful, you will win some unfaithful friends and some genuine enemies. Succeed anyway.

21

4. If you are honest and sincere people may deceive you. Be honest and sincere anyway.

5. What you spend years creating, others could destroy overnight. Create anyway.

6. If you find serenity and happiness, some may be jealous. Be happy anyway.

7. The good you do today, will often be forgotten. Do good anyway.

8. Give the best you have, and it will never be enough. Give your best anyway.

9. In the final analysis, it is between you and God. It was never between you and them anyway.

David's Prayer for Pardon and Confession of Sin

(Psalm 51, WEB)

Have mercy on me, God, according to your loving kindness. According to the multitude of your tender mercies, blot out my transgressions. Wash me thoroughly from my iniquity. Cleanse me from my sin. For I know my transgressions. My sin is constantly before me. Against you, and you only, have I sinned, and done that which is evil in your sight; that you may be proved right when you speak, and justified when you judge. Behold, I was brought forth in iniquity. In sin my mother conceived me. Behold, you desire truth in the inward parts. You teach me wisdom in the inmost place. Purify me with hyssop, and I will be clean. Wash me, and I will be whiter than snow. Let me hear joy and gladness, That the bones which you have broken may rejoice

Hide your face from my sins, and blot out all of my iniquities.

Create in me a clean heart, O God. Renew a right spirit within me. Don't throw me from your presence, and don't take your holy Spirit from me. Restore to me the joy of your salvation. Uphold me with a willing spirit. Then I will teach transgressors your ways. Sinners shall be converted to you. Deliver me from bloodguiltiness, O God, the God of my salvation. My tongue shall sing aloud of your righteousness. Lord, open my lips. My mouth shall declare your praise. For you don't delight in sacrifice, or else I would give it. You have no pleasure in burnt offering. The sacrifices of God are a broken spirit. A broken and contrite heart, O God, you will not despise. Do well in your good pleasure to Zion. Build the walls of Jerusalem. Then you will delight in the sacrifices of righteousness, in burnt offerings and in whole burnt offerings. Then they will offer bulls on your altar.

Reflections

Reflections

Day 4...
Prayer Hand

"Let us therefore draw near with boldness to the throne of grace, that we may receive mercy, and may find grace for help in time of need" (Hebrews 4:16, WEB)

Back then, when I was a teacher in church, I loved teaching this one to the little ones during Sunday School. We would outline their hands and guide them through the prayer. I even became unusual in my approach one time and wrote the ideas on a rubber glove to wear while teaching the lesson. You don't have to do all that fancy stuff, though.

Trace around your open hand to create an outline hand in your prayer journal. Write a prayer for each finger:

Thumb – Pray for those close to you (family and friends).

Pointer Finger – Pray for teachers, instructors, doctors, ministers, etc.

Tall Finger – Pray for those in charge, that is, President, government officials, state leaders, city leaders, etc.

Ring Finger – Pray for those who are weak (the sick, those in trouble or pain, etc.).

Little Finger – Pray for yourself and your needs.

Reflections

Day 5...
Thank You List to God

"Yahweh, in the morning you shall hear my voice. In the morning I will lay my requests before you, and will watch expectantly." (Psalm 5:3, WEB)

Set your timer for 10 minutes and write your list of everyday things for which you are thankful. Be very specific and write everything you can think of and everything you can see. When the time is up, spend 5 minutes praying your thanks to God.

Reflections

Day 6...
Pray The Scriptures

"For the word of God is living, and active, and sharper than any two-edged sword, and piercing even to the dividing of soul and spirit, of both joints and marrow, and quick to discern the thoughts and intents of the heart." (Hebrews 4:12, ASV)

The disciples came to Christ and asked Him to teach them to pray. The New Testament, originally written in Greek used the word 'teach' and it meant to 'instruct or to cause to learn.' What has blessed me most is that it also meant 'to teach the scriptures.'

The disciples weren't just asking Christ to teach them how to pray, they were asking Him to teach them how to pray in a way that would be pleasing to God, a way that would be results as desired. Why?

It may be my twisted sense of humor, but I think it had to do with the ending story in Luke 10. It's the famous story of Martha and Mary. Christ had come to their house, and Martha got miffed at Mary. Martha was busy doing all the tasks needed to entertain the visitors. She watched Mary who sat at Jesus' feet, wondering why she would have to bear the burden all alone. Martha complained to Christ about her lack of help but Jesus gently rebuked her anger. He said that Mary was doing the good thing.

I can just imagine that they walked away from the dinner at Martha and Mary's house a little concerned. Jesus rebuked Martha (the busy one), and Mary was the good one (doing the listening.) Don't you know that the disciples didn't want to make the same mistake? It's after this scene that Jesus was praying and the disciples asked Him to teach them to pray.

Praying the Scriptures is a powerful and meaningful way to pray. In Hebrews 4:12, the Bible says that the word of God is living, active, and powerful. Speaking and praying the Scriptures allows us to come into agreement with God because we are praying His words back to Him..

Do you feel like you're stuck on what to pray for about a situation? Or maybe you feel like God doesn't hear your scatterbrained prayers. You can rest assured you are in line with His will when you are praying His Holy words found in the Scriptures.

Praying the scriptures will help your spiritual growth as you learn what God says about certain situations. When you pray the scriptures, they become planted in your heart.

You can use a concordance in your Bible or the Internet to search for a scripture on your topic of need. Then, rewrite the scripture inserting names where appropriate. When you pray, you'll simply pray the rewritten scripture back to God. It's the format I used when I created the 'Coloring Prayer Journal: 30 Days of Praying Scripture Over Your Adult Children' for my mom.

Reflections

Reflections

Day 7...
Letters to God

"Hear my prayer, O Jehovah; give ear to my supplications: In thy faithfulness answer me, and in thy righteousness." (Psalm 143:1, ASV)

Pray your heart and spill your guts. That's the best advice I can give to anyone that wants to write a prayer letter to God. Your letter to God is a way to pour your heart out just the way you would write a letter to a dear friend.

The most important things to remember:

- Pour your heart out.
- Don't hold back.
- Don't write and erase. Just let it be.

Reflections

Day 8...
Adore and Praise God

"Let the words of my mouth and the meditation of my heart be acceptable in your sight, Yahweh, my rock, and my redeemer." (Psalm 19:14, WEB)

I like to do this prayer with a 15 minute timer. Write a prayer of love, adoration and praise to God. Think of every name and phrase that describes your Heavenly Father and why that speaks to your heart. Earlier on, I talked of prayer as romance with God. Couples in a given marriage relationship adore each other by using sweet words to describe their mutual feelings. Adore Him, too. Praise Him for who He is to you.

Reflections

Day 9...
Prayer of Praise

"I cried to him with my mouth. He was extolled with my tongue."
(Psalm 66:17, WEB)

In the previous section, I said you should praise God for who He is to you. In the case of the prayer of praise, you have something different a bit. Write a prayer of Praise to God for two specific two things He has accomplished in your life. Be very specific with as many details as you can remember. Praise Him for what He has done.

Remember this one thing: Your mind is powerful and is influenced by your mouth. If you say enough negative things, your mind will start to believe that negativity. Writing and saying praise and adoration over things God has accomplished in your life is mighty. It reinforces and strengthens your faith.

Reflections

Day 10...
Music to the Soul

"Hear my prayer, O Jehovah; give ear to my supplications: In thy

faithfulness answer me, and in thy righteousness." (Psalm 143:1, ASV)

Play a favorite praise and worship song, and write your prayer from it. As you listen to the words of the song, your heart can be moved to write your heartfelt prayers while being lifted up by the music. I like to do this by listening to about three or four songs in a row and letting my praises and prayers flow with the music. |Experiences have shown that playing spiritual, edifying music can create an atmosphere of worship around you as you sing along.

Reflections

Day 11...
Pray For Your Enemies

"Love your enemies and pray for those who persecute you" (Matthew 5:44, WEB)

"But I tell you who hear: love your enemies, do good to those who hate you, bless those who curse you, and pray for those who mistreat you" (Luke 6:27-28, WEB)

Whether someone persecutes, abuses, hates, or curses us, we are to pray for them, be it people whose violations are minimally annoying or very physically hurtful, or perhaps loved ones we don't think of as enemies but who sometimes act as if they are. Forgive others even if it were a mortal enemy trying to find a way to end our life.

What can you pray when you are praying for your enemies—the people who treat you badly? A good place to start is to pray the way you pray for yourself, not only for their physical needs but also their eternal needs.

Today, choose an enemy and write a heartfelt prayer to God. Pray for their earthly needs (food, clothing, housing, transportation, etc.) and also pray for their eternal needs (a repentant heart, grace to show mercy, ability to extend love, as well as protection from temptations and the destructive power of Satan.)

A long time ago, I heard a minister say that you can't stay mad at someone if you are praying for them. That's because the emotion of anger and goodwill are on the opposite ends of the emotional spectrum. So, let's get real here. There are events, instances, and people that are our enemies. They are out to destroy us, make us feel unworthy, and tear us down. However, Christ's response to us is that we should pray for them. I know it can be hard. But remember, *"we can do all things through Christ who gives us the strength"* (Philippians 4:13). I think that includes praying for our enemies too.

Reflections

Day 12...
Take a Prayer Walk

"Now it happened, when all the people were baptized, Jesus also had been baptized, and was praying. The sky was opened, and the Holy Spirit descended in a bodily form as a dove on him; and a voice came out of the sky, saying "You are my beloved Son. In you I am well pleased." (Luke 3:21-22, WEB)

In the scripture above, you read about several scenes of nature. Jesus was baptized in a river. So I can imagine the sounds of the water as people walked down into it for their baptism. I can as well hear the sound of the river as people came up after having been baptized with their clothes turned wet in the water. People were milling about, so I'm sure there was a hum of voices. Then we get the visual scene of the sky opening up and a dove descending on Christ. Finally, we hear the voice of God. There were so many sights and sounds to be thankful for that day.

Take a walk outside and pray a prayer of thanks for everything you see. Pay attention to every little and big thing! Be safe while walking, which means no walking and writing. It's a mental prayer today. Also, rather than trying to remember everything later, just note in your Prayer Journal 'Prayer Walk' with the date and the weather conditions. That's all! Now, why should you do this as part of your prayer ideas? God reveals Himself in creation, as you can learn about His attributes through things around you (See Romans 1:20).

Reflections

Day 13...
Pray Your To-Do List

"I beseech you therefore, brethren, by the mercies of God, to present your bodies a living sacrifice, holy, acceptable to God, which is your spiritual service." (Romans 12:1, ASV)

Use your weekly to-do list to focus on your prayer needs for the week ahead of you. Think about the places and situations you will be in, the people you will meet and the challenges you may face. Pray through these things asking God to be with you.

You can use these questions as prayer prompts:

- Where will I spend my days?

- What will my main challenges be?

- What people will I meet?

- What are other prayer concerns for this week?

Reflections

Day 14...
The Three Circles

"In my distress I called upon Jehovah, And cried unto my God: He heard my voice out of his temple, And my cry before him came into his ears." (Psalm 18:6, ASV)

Draw three circles, like you see on a target on the dartboard or archer bull's eye. Be sure to make it as large as your paper, because you'll be writing names inside. Label the inner circle with "My Neighborhood" and then write in names of your neighbors and local situations that need prayer. Then, draw another outer circle and label it "My Country" and write in issues within your country that are in need of prayer. Lastly, draw the larger outer circle and label it "Other Countries" and make notes of international events that need prayer.

Take some time to pray over the names in your circles.

Reflections

Day 15...
Lectio Divina

"But you, when you pray, enter into your inner room, and having shut your door, pray to your Father who is in secret, and your Father who sees in secret will reward you openly" (Matthew 6:6, WEB)

Lectio Divina is a Latin term meaning "divine reading," and it describes a way of reading the Scriptures slowly with much meditation and thought. It's traced back to a 12th-century monk who taught the key stages involved in the process as follows (comments in parenthesis are my notes):

First, you read your selected verse slowly and reflectively so that it can sink in. Use any passage of Scripture but don't make it too long. (While not mandatory, I like to use one verse.)

The second stage is the reflection time where you think about the scripture. (I like to read it multiple times, three or four times very slowly.)

The third stage is your response. (This is where you have to put aside your personal thinking and let God speak to your heart. Write down your thoughts word by word. What does God impress on you?)

The final stage is to rest in God. (It's important to do this prayer time in a quiet environment so that you can hear God's gentle whispers during the stillness of your meditation.)

Reflections

Day 16...
Pray and Answer Prayers

"For where two or three are gathered together in my name, there I am in the midst of them" (Matthew 18:20, WEB)

Pray and answer prayers refers to the old list system. I still like to keep this list, but I just don't pray the format every single day. By keeping a side-by-side prayer list, you will be able to keep track of the results of your prayers. Seeing results encourages your prayerful spirit.

To set this up in your journal, you draw a line through the middle of the page. On the left side, write the date and the prayer request. On the left corresponding side, you will write the result of the prayer. Soon, you will start seeing God's answers to some of the prayers. It will be an encouragement to you as you continue to see God's faithfulness in answering your prayers.

Note: This should be a page in your journal that you can visit daily or weekly to keep up with the prayer items. I like to put a paper clip on this page so that I can find it easily.

Reflections

Day 17...
The Teaspoon Prayer

"Rejoicing in hope; enduring in troubles; continuing steadfastly in prayer" (Romans 12:12, WEB)

The Teaspoon Prayer is an entry in your prayer journal inspired by the little teaspoon in your silverware drawer. The abbreviation for teaspoon is tsp, and it goes like this:

T is for ***Thank You.***

S is for ***Sorry.***

P is for ***Please***.

Write a **T** at the top of the page and list things that you thank God for today. When you are ready to move on, place an **S** on the page. Write and pray to God the things that you need to say sorry for. Once you've finished the sorry stage, you write a **P** on the page. Write the things that you are asking God for.

Reflections

Day 18...
Sermon Notes Prayers

"In the same way, the Spirit also helps our weaknesses, for we don't know how to pray as we ought. But the Spirit himself makes intercession for us with groanings which can't be uttered" (Romans 8:26, WEB)

Sermon Notes Prayers deal with the use of your sermon notes from your weekly church service. Of course, this is assuming that you take notes. I highly suggest the practice of taking notes during the entire service. Most church services include times of praise & worship, sharing of prayer needs, and the minister's sermon. Pray for the minister, the leaders, and the people and their needs; review the songs, scriptures, and notes and let them inspire your prayer. Reread the scriptures and specifically, pray about how they can influence your life for a change.

Reflections

Day 19...
Prayer Collage

"I called upon the LORD in distress: the LORD answered me, and set me in a large place" (Psalm 118:5, KJV)

Sometimes words fail us. Even in something as simple as prayer we just can't find the words to say. It may also be that our minds are just so full of the cares of this world that we find it hard to concentrate.

In times like these, I find a very soothing way to pray, which is the prayer collage. I put some encouraging praise music on and grab a couple of magazines I don't mind destroying. With the soothing praise and worship music playing in the background, I then go through the pages and cut out pictures and words that speak to my soul. After about 30 minutes of cutting and gluing, I find that the collage created soothes my spirit. I then write a prayer thanking God for the specific things He spoke to me while I creatively prayed. I usually allow about 30 minutes to an hour to do this creative prayer idea.

Reflections

Day 20...
Prayer Graffiti

"Call to me, and I will answer you, and will show you great things, and difficult, which you don't know" (Jeremiah 33:3, WEB)

Choose a designated space in your home and mount a large poster board, long paper or even a blank piece of copy paper. You can write your prayers, drawings, or verses on the 'wall.' If it's in a public place in the house, invite other family members to join you. After a month, rejoice over all your prayerful graffiti.

Reflections

Day 21...
A.M./P.M. Prayers

"Yet the LORD will command his loving kindness in the daytime, and in the night his song shall be with me, and my prayer unto the God of my life" (Psalm 42:8, KJV)

The day you do this creative prayer time, you'll have two prayer times that I find work very well together. Whenever I have my prayer time in this format, God usually speaks wonderful messages to me.

During the A.M. prayers:

Write your prayers to God using one of these creative prayer ideas:

Be prayerFULL (Day 1)

Pray the Scriptures (Day 6)

Letters to God (Day 7)

During your P.M. prayers:

Spend 15 minutes listening to worship music and write your prayers as described in the Prayer of Praise idea. It never ceases to amaze me how God uses music in the evening that speaks directly to what I have prayed in the morning.

Reflections

Bonus:
More Creative Prayer & Journal Ideas

Prayer Poster

Tape four envelopes to a small piece of pasteboard that will fit on your fridge or kitchen cabinet. Have a pen and some index cards nearby. On the other four envelopes, write the words, ***Praise***, ***Thanks***, ***Forgive***, and ***Please help***. If a prayer idea occurs, write it on an index card and slip it in the appropriate envelope. You can pray through the cards at a selected time of day or day of the week.

Shredding or Burning Your Prayers

Here is a powerful but noisy or smelly way to illustrate the act of giving your prayer over to God. It's a way of saying, "I rest my case," like the attorney in a courtroom. We could say it's one way of casting your care on God with no chances of ever picking it up again—at least in your mind (1 Peter 5:7). You just let it be that God may take charge. Write your prayer on paper, then run it through the shredder or burn it. It's an effective way to pray when you have a heavy burden that you need to release to God.

Portable Prayer List

Do you ever look at your desk and see you have a pile of business cards you've collected from businesses? You hate to throw them away because you may need them, but for now, they aren't doing you any service. You can turn your stack into a portable prayer list. Write a name or a topic on each one and wrap a rubber band around them or put them in a snack size bag. When you are waiting in a long line, riding the bus or train or out for your daily walk, you can work your way through the stack.

Picture Prayer Wall

All those photos yet how many are still on your phone? Print out or have them printed and use them to create your prayer wall. You can tape them to a poster board, put them on the fridge, our pin them on a cork board. Put them somewhere where you'll see them regularly. Use them as your inspiration to pray for those people.

Old Fashioned Pity Party

Just let it out. Have an old fashioned pity party by writing out all your complaints, fears, bad things, and life gone wrong things to God. It's O.K. It is! If you read some of the Psalms, that's what David did, and he's considered a "man after God's own heart."

3 - Ring Binder

You can't get any easier than a -inch 3-Ring Binder and some loose leaf notebook paper to make your journal. You can divide your journal up into days so that you can look back on your prayer journal by the days of the week. Alternatively, you can make a section for each of the prayer journal ideas by their categories. Then add those prayers by section. You could even add more sections for personal journaling, Bible study notes, doodles, and inspired thoughts. If keeping your prayers in sequential order in a notebook isn't fancy enough then the 3-ring binder method may be the way for you.

Note Cards

I use note cards for my to-do list and outlining books, so I have lots of note cards in our house. I use them to write out Bible verses. I also like to put specific names on them when I know I'm going to spend my prayer time while walking. You can punch a hole in the corner and then use a binder ring, a big rubber band, or binder clip to keep them all together. I prefer a binder ring.

Smartphone or Tablet

I'm a little old-fashioned and like to keep my prayer journaling with pen or pencil and paper. But, if you want, you can use your mobile devices like a phone, tablet or computer. With apps like Google Drive, Notes, and Evernote, you can categorize your prayer journal electronically.

Conclusion: Pray, Sister, Pray!

I first learned to pray when I was a young preteen growing up in the church. Until that time, I had been to church a few times. However, the times were so few I hardly knew what prayer was.

As the years have rolled by, I find myself in the season of life called the "Fall" years. However, I don't know if it's my age or the times in which we are living. Either way, I find myself with a new fervency to pray and to encourage other women to cultivate their prayer lives.

I've taught you a lot of different ways to have meaningful conversations with God in this book. More than you realize.

You'll never mark praying off your list as ultimately completed. It's true. You'll never be done needing to prepare your heart for new things in life. There is no perfect time here on earth when prayer won't be needed. You'll never be completely ready for what craziness life may throw at you. But, you can minimize your sad, nervous or hopeless feelings. You can encourage others. You can help yourself and others. All through the power of prayer.

About the Author

Kim C. Steadman has ministered alongside her family since 1977, and with her husband since 1984. After working in the private sector for 16 years, God turned her heart towards home. In the sanctuary of her little cottage in Texas with her husband and fur-child, she now fulfills a childhood dream of writing. Her passion is to encourage empty-nest women to say 'yes' to themselves. The motto of her blog is to repurpose and redesign your life with God as your Master Designer. Find out more about Kim at her website, www.KimSteadman.com. She also enjoys doodle drawing, crafts, DIY projects, hiking and planning adventures for her grandson.

APPENDIX

Scripture Index

Other Resources

Prayer Study with Coloring Pages:

I created a companion prayer study to enhance your prayer journey. The three-week studies are titled:
- Design Your Prayer Space
- Praying Like Jesus
- Define Your Desires

The study includes a printable set of all the scriptures included in this book, along with the weekly study and a coloring page I designed to enhance your mediation. You can download the prayer study here:

www.KimSteadman.com/study

My Favorite Books on Prayer:

My walk with God sometimes feels like I'm dragging my feet through thick mud. It's not God's fault. I'm the one with the struggles, the hang-ups, the imperfections. But, it's nothing a little prayer won't fix. I have some favorite books about prayer. You can find my list here:

www.KimSteadman.com/prayer

60551174R00048

Made in the USA
Lexington, KY
10 February 2017